Pathways to HOPE AND HEALING

TEACHER'S GUIDE

Pathways to HOPE AND HEALING

Healing the Lasting Effects of Prolonged Stress, Trauma and Dysfunction

TEACHER'S GUIDE

MILLIE MCCARTY, M.A., LPCC-S

Pathways to Hope and Healing: Teacher's Guide

Copyright © 2023 by Millie McCarty, M.A., LPCC-S

No portion of this book may be reproduced, stored in a retrieval system, or transmitted in any form by any means—electronic, mechanical, photocopy, recording, or other—except for brief quotations in printed reviews, without prior permission of the author.

Requests for information should be addressed to:
The Healing Hub at the Gate
Pickerington, Ohio 43147
milliehealinghub4u@gmail.com

Paperback ISBN: 978-1-7354796-2-0

Table of Contents

Preface	Author Bio, Purpose, Goals	vii
Lesson One:	Changing Times	1
Lesson Two:	Where the Battle Begins	3
Lesson Three:	Family Tree—Getting to the Root	5
Lesson Four:	Family Systems—Laying the Foundation	7
Lesson Five:	Families Make a Difference	9
Lesson Six:	Growing Up In Stages:	11
Lesson Seven:	Taking The Ax to the Root	13
Lesson Eight:	Walls We Build	15
Lesson Nine:	Web of Lies	17
Lesson Ten:	Lies, Oaths, and Vows	19
Lesson Eleven:	Out of Darkness	20
Lesson Twelve:	Cycle of Sin and Addiction/ Iceberg Theory	22
Lesson Thirteen:	Healthy Boundaries	25
Lesson Fourteen:	Breaking Free	27
Lesson Fifteen:	Renewing the Mind	29
Personal Inventory Questionnaire		32
References List		37

Millie McCarty, M.A., LPCC-S—Graduating Cum Laude from Defiance College with a B. A. Degree in Religious Education, Millie went on to receive her M.A. degree in Guidance and Counseling from The Ohio State University in 1981 and became a Licensed Professional Clinical Counselor in 1985. Millie's background as a Director of Education at her church and a Parenting Educator as well as a Personal Growth & Development Trainer added to the richness of her knowledge and ability to meet people where their need was.

Widely known in Ohio as a counselor and teacher, Millie served 20 years as the founder and Executive Director of Lighthouse Counseling Services from 1981–2001, when she retired to write and teach. Her groundbreaking work in the areas of early childhood sexual, ritual abuse, and dissociative identity disorder, has brought healing and restoration through her strategic, systematic design combining faith principles and proven professional strategies to thousands of adult victims of childhood sexual trauma to citizens of Ohio.

After retiring, Millie began a ten-year journey of co-writing a case study entitled *"RUTH: Secret of the Silenced Voices;"—A Guide to Working with People with Dissociative Identity Disorders."* During this period from 2002–2012, as a by-product of the case study, Millie wrote her next book *"WHY WE CAN'T Just Get Over It"— Healing the Effects of Prolonged Stress and Trauma*. At the same time, developing her "Systematic Process" of resolving unresolved conflicts needed for restoration. Millie began being asked to train people from other nations such as China, Ethiopia, Jamaica, Finland, Haiti, Rwanda, Uganda, and Cuba. Today she is being called to train church leaders at home and abroad in her Systematic Process to equip the church for the great harvest that lies before us.

Why We Can't Just Get Over It was written because of a ten-year assignment to write a Case Study *RUTH: Secrets of the Silenced Voices;* the story of the life of one lady who had experienced a lifetime of abuse and trauma at the hands of her father's live-in friend who was a pedophile. Her life included every kind of abuse and torture including Satanic Ritual Abuse, yet she went on to be functional as a schoolteacher and executive employee in the State Dept. of Social Services as well as maintaining a strong belief in God. Ruth lived to tell her story and assist Millie in teaching the first class of *RUTH* and *Why We Can't Just Get Over It* in China twice and Ethiopia before going home to her eternal peace in 2017.

Systematic Process for Resolving Unresolved Conflict Eternally (SPRUCE)

From 2012–2017 Millie implemented a systematic approach to equipping others with the tools to provide care for survivors of abuse and trauma using her curriculum and implementing other coursework to provide the necessary skills to restore the life skills missed during the time of abuse and trauma. Based on her 35 years of counseling and training, these classes were established as a certification program. Her goal is to get the curriculum accredited and published to provide all nations with this *Systematic Process of Resolving Unresolved Conflict Eternal (SPRUCE)*.

This **HEALING THE HEART** course was designed specifically to take to the nations. It contains excerpts from *"PATHWAYS TO HOPE AND HEALING,"* Copyright©2002 and *"WHY WE CAN'T "JUST GET OVER IT"*, Copyright ©2009, both written by Millie McCarty, M.A., LPCC. All rights reserved. No part of this publication may be reproduced, transmitted in any form, or stored in a retrieval system without prior written permission of the author, except in the case of brief quotations embodied in articles and previews. Requests for information should be addressed to (e-mail: milliehealinghub4u@gmail.com).

CONTENT AND GOALS: Healing the Heart is a composite of both books developed by founder and CEO, Millie McCarty, MA., LPCC-Supervisor; "Pathways to Hope and Healing" and "Why We Can't Just Get Over It". To bring the core teachings of INT'L INSTITUTE FOR TRAUMA RECOVERY ministry, we have chosen the most important sections of these two books to accomplish the following goals:

- To train participants in the systematic use of eight assessment tools that assist in getting to the root issues beneath the surface of the mental, emotional, and behavioral signs of stress and trauma. Once the roots have been uncovered, we learn how to do "Spiritual Surgery" to literally "take the ax to the root" … rooting out the lies and replacing them with God's Truth…. thus, facilitating their healing from trauma. The Teacher's Guide is also used to train leaders in the systematic approach to healing survivors of abuse and trauma using Millie McCarty's unique SPRUCE process.
- To help participants apply the Biblical principles of healing to their trauma-based thoughts, emotions, and actions.
- To begin to understand the amazing neurological connection between the brain and gut and the power of our thoughts over our body's system that is designed to protect us; and how to begin to direct that energy and power in such a way that it brings healing instead of disease.

LESSON ONE: CHANGING TIMES

GOALS: Identifying the evolution of the American Family and its effects on our children and nation.

PREPARATION: Set up tables in such a way that they can see each other (round tables) or long tables so all can see the speaker/PowerPoint screen. Round tables are best for table discussions. If long tables are used, make sure the people can sit across from each other and look eye to eye…so each person can be drawn in visually and audibly by the group. If possible, have a facilitator at each table (a facilitator is someone who has been through the class before and can lead the group through the class activities.
- The teacher introduces him/herself, then the name of the class, and describes the goals of the class.
- Lesson One is a time to introduce curriculum purpose and goals. See pgs.ix–x (Use book/PPT)
- Share CLASS BLESSING (on PPT or on a sign or handout). See pg.31 in Teacher's Guide.
- Icebreaker—Give each person a chance to introduce him/herself and where they come from…and perhaps what they hope to get out of the group.

CHANGING TIMES….is a look at major changes that took place in America during the 1960s to the 1980s…changes that impacted individual choices, the health of the family, and the stability of the Country. CHANGING TIMES booklets available for purchase. See website: https://healinghub.wpengine.com/.

JOEL:
- FUTURE WAR OF THE CHURCH
- THE CALL FOR THE CHURCH TO ARISE IN THE YEAR 2000.
- THE COMING CHURCH REVOLUTION
- AUTHORITY QUESTIONED: MAN'S WAYS OR GOD'S WAYS??? MAN: GOD'S CREATION OR EVOLVING FROM ANIMAL…REBELLION AGAINST GOD and GOD'S WORD
- THE GOD IS DEAD MOVEMENT
- Snatch from the Fire: Jude 1:22-23
- THE COMING HARVEST

PRINCIPALITIES OVER NATIONS: Wars, soldiers, and families without fathers; see pgs.2, 11, 12.

NOAH: Rebellious nature—Divisive Principalities; see pgs.11–12.
- Have the group divide into small groups to study the divisive nature of principalities.
- Each group will be given the name and type of principality to study.
- And create a skit to portray the effects on others of the actions of each principality.

TABLE ACTIVITY—*PRINCIPALITIES OVER FAMILIES AND NATIONS:* See pgs.11–12.
Directions: Give each table the name and description of a principality—have participants study scripture that defines the nature of the principality they received and develop a two-minute illustration (skit) of what this principality would look like.

REFLECTIVE EXERCISES: *Principalities Over Families and Nations*—Make note of how many of the above characteristics you recognize in your family, community, business, school, media, and people around you. How do they influence your thinking and behavior?

SUMMARIZE THE LESSON and DISCUSS QUESTIONS: See pgs. 13–14.
CLOSING PRAYER

Complete: GROUP COUNSELING NOTE to identify what they have learned in this session.
HOMEWORK: Read over material for next lesson.

PRINCIPALITIES OVER FAMILIES AND NATIONS

"For we wrestle not against flesh and blood, but against principalities, against powers, against the rulers of the darkness of this world, against spiritual wickedness in high places."—Ephesians 6:12

Hivites: Were known for discrediting and slander; repeating matters outside of proper channels of authority and relations and tale-bearing. (I Peter 4:15)

Perizzites: Were known for division and contention, setting up ambushes to cause fighting against each other. (Matthew 12:25)

Jebusites: Were known for their filth, uncleanness, and sexual immorality. (II Peter 2:9-10, Romans 6:18-20, I Thessalonians 4:3-7)

Girgashites: Were a people known for anxiety and worry—a basic distrust of God and unbelief. (Hebrews 3:19) Their cares are choked because of their lack of trust in God. (Matthew 13:22)

Hittites: Were known for their discouragement, complaining, and murmuring which brings on depression and despondency. (Moses: Numbers 11:10-15); (Elijah: 1 Kings 19:1-9); (Disciples: John 6:58-60)

Canaanites: Were known for their superiority; making people feel inferior, paranoid, fearful, overwhelmed, intimidated, and rejected (Numbers 13:33)

Amorites: Were prideful, arrogant, self-centered, and unteachable, and delighted in finding defects in leadership. (Numbers 21:13, Psalms 73:6-9, Proverbs 8:13, Proverbs 16:18, Proverbs 29:22) —Author Unknown

LESSON TWO: WHERE THE BATTLE BEGINS

Review: Cultural changes—CHANGING TIMES—WAR AGAINST GOD…EVOLUTION

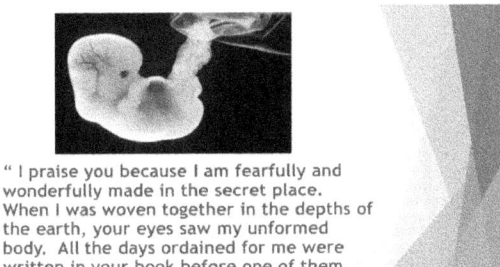

" I praise you because I am fearfully and wonderfully made in the secret place. When I was woven together in the depths of the earth, your eyes saw my unformed body. All the days ordained for me were written in your book before one of them came to be."

Updated statistics from CHANGING TIMES—2019
- Beliefs/ perceptions and actions that have resulted in negative consequences of rebellion against God in America.
- Abortion, Divorce, Sexual issues, Sex addiction, AIDS/other diseases
- Alcohol, drugs, drug addiction
- Medical Model—Medication (drugs),
- Spiritual (foreign gods/ancient beliefs (astrology, tarot cards, tea leaves, psychic powers, transcendental meditation).

CHURCH: More like the world

God's protection: Armor of God
- Put on the Armor of God—Description of the Armor of God
- Link together—follow God's commands to defeat the enemies of God.
- Purpose and power; see next page.
- Discuss questions; see pgs.13–14.
- Prayer for Repentance and Confession of Faith; see pg.15.
- Equipping for Warfare
  - Holy Spirit
  - God's Word
  - Armor of God

HOMEWORK: Complete Personal Inventory Questionnaire. See pgs.140–146. Also, identify signs/symptoms of trauma. (Do this as homework and bring it to the group next time). Study scriptures regarding types of prayer. Read over material for the next lesson.

Complete: GROUP COUNSELING NOTE to identify what they have learned in this session.

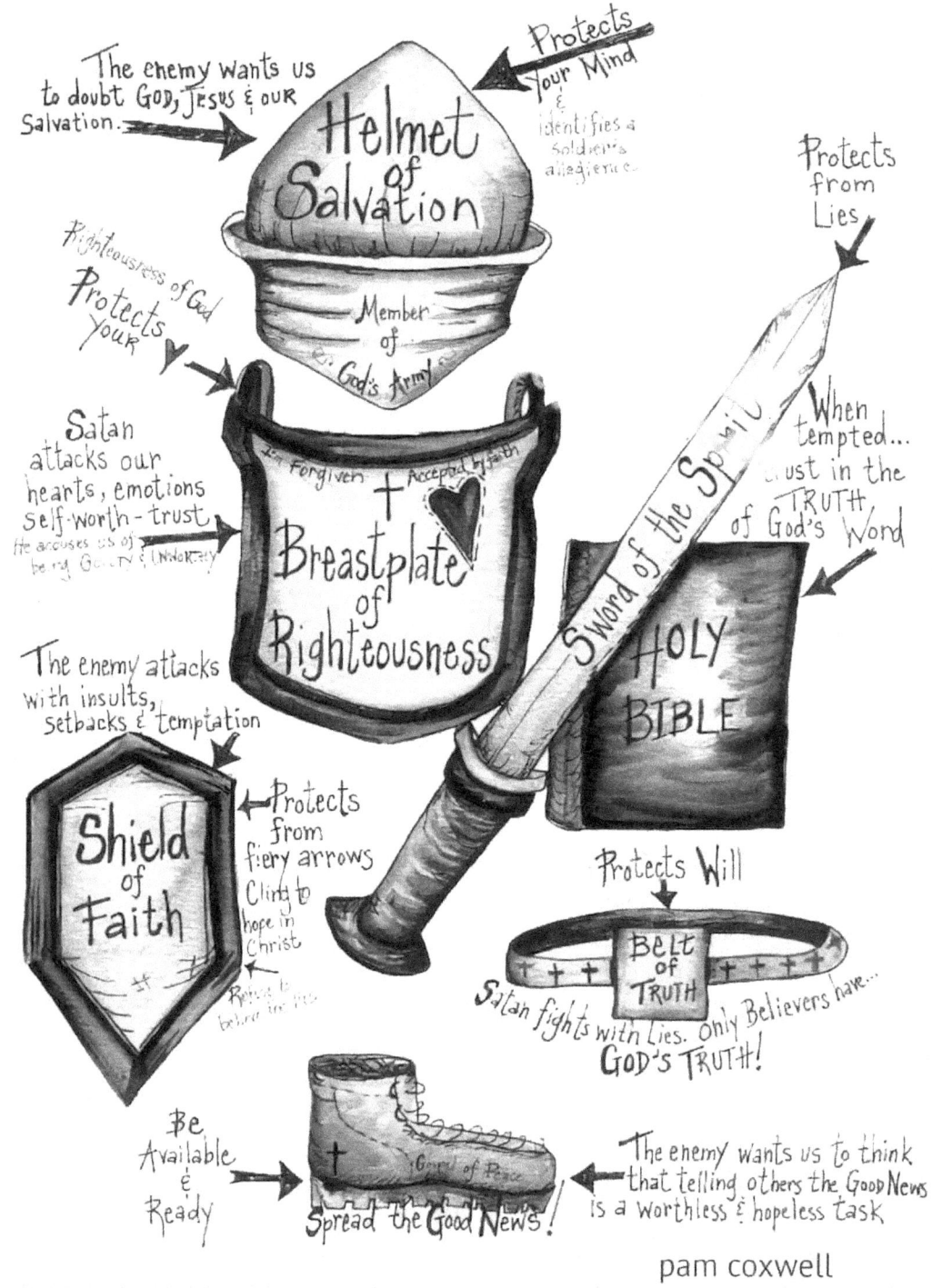

LESSON THREE: FAMILY TREE—GETTING TO THE ROOT

FAMILY ROOTS: Share baby in the womb.
- Five Senses (slide or picture)—Mental, physical, emotional health of mother (body, mind, and spirit) transmits through skin, tissue, umbilical cord which is the neurological system connecting baby to mother and (DNA) of mother and father.

INSTRUCTIONS FOR PARENTS: Words, looks, smells, touch, all communicate what their world is like—safe, unsafe, trusting/non-trusting, peaceful/ chaotic; see Deut. 5-6.

INCLUSION, CONTROL, AFFECT: All communicated through five senses—bonding stages—Every child needs to be loved and wanted…also need to trust to grow.

WORDS HAVE POWER: Proverbs 12:18, Isaiah 51:12-16

ESTABLISHING BONDING & HEALTHY RELATIONSHIPS:

REVIEW TREE OF BONDAGE VS. TREE OF FREEDOM: See pg.25.

REFLECTIVE EXERCISE: Ask God to shed His light on your tree. What does the fruit of your tree tell you about family roots? See pg.24.

TABLE ACTIVITY: Share what you see/experienced in your family that made you who you are… What does your fruit look like? What were your roots like? What does the fruit tell you about your family tree?

ESTABLISHING BONDING AND HEALTHY RELATIONSHIPS

"Make a tree good and its fruit will be good, or make a tree bad and its fruit will be bad, for a tree recognized by its fruit." - Matthew 12:33

In order to bond with one another and to establish healthy relationships, children need to know they have the following components to family life::

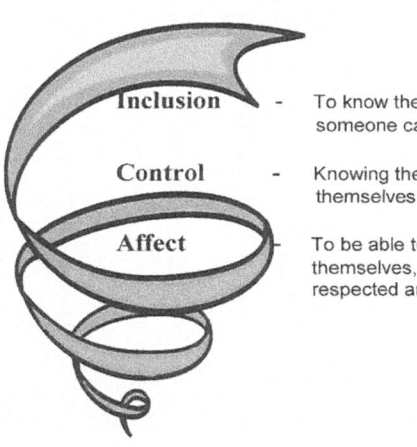

- **Inclusion** - To know they are loved, safe, protected, secure, that someone cares for them
- **Control** - Knowing they can master daily activities, and help themselves do what they see others doing.
- **Affect** - To be able to affect change in the situation they find themselves, and know their ideas and thoughts are respected and contribute to making a difference.

Review: FAMILY SYSTEMS MODEL
Homework: Read over material for the next lesson.
COMPLETE: GROUP COUNSELING NOTE to identify what they have learned in this lesson.

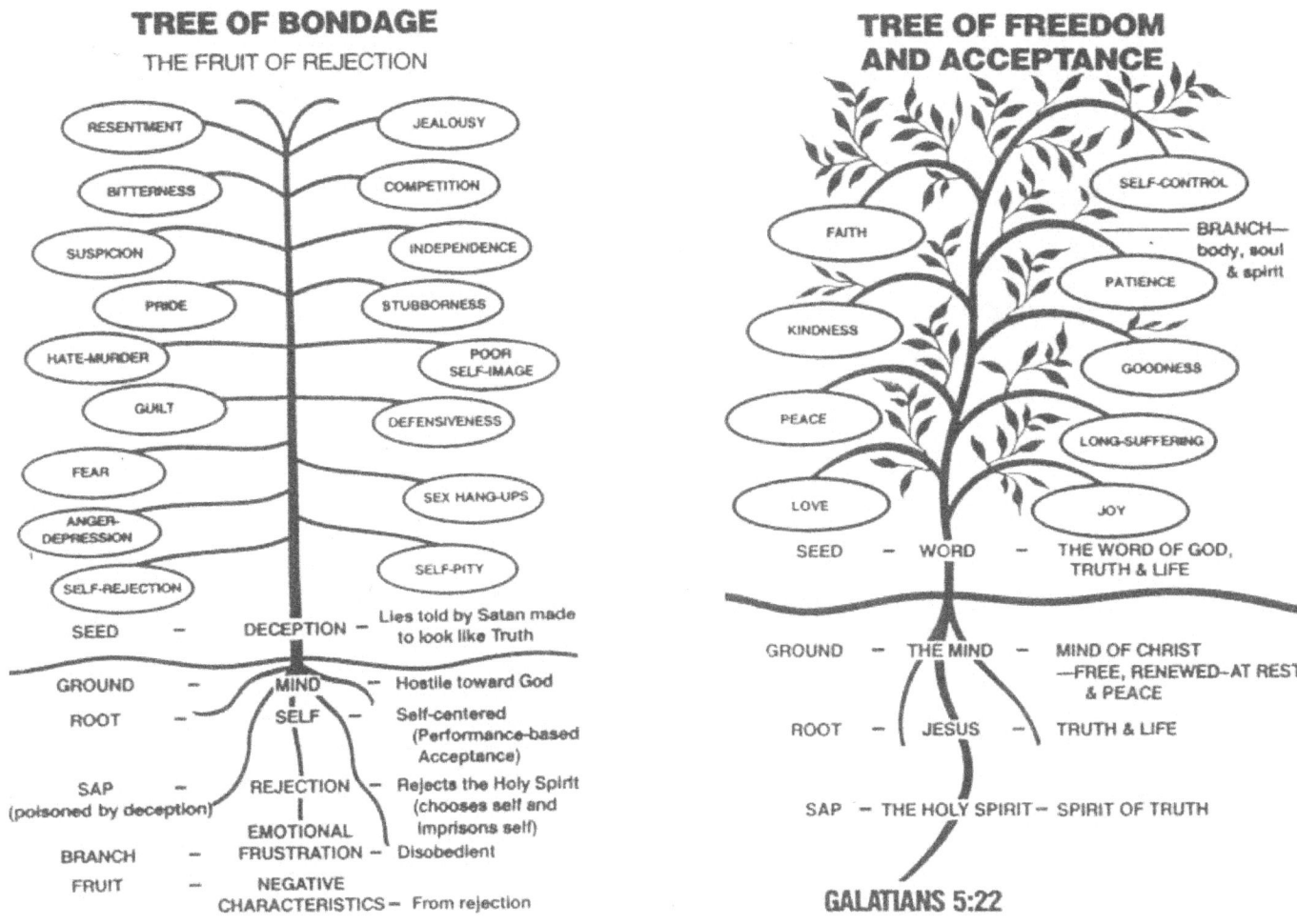

SOURCE UNKNOWN

*"God's Word is living and active ...and His word conveys TRUTH...
When His light is shed on our beliefs, it is like a two-edged sword."* —Hebrews 4:12-13

LESSON FOUR: FAMILY SYSTEMS—LAYING THE FOUNDATION

FAMILY SYSTEMS MODEL—GOD'S DESIGN: Rules, Roles, Rituals (routines), Standards, Beliefs, Values

WORLD INFLUENCES: Education, Entertainment, Religion, Media, Economy, Government

FORMATION PROCESS takes place through family interaction and prepares children to go out into the world to take their place in society. God has a plan for every child.

GOD'S PLAN FOR FAMILY: DEUTERONOMY 5-6

EARLY AMERICA—Govt. founded on biblical principles: All schools, colleges, hospitals, mental health hospitals, children's homes, care for the homeless, sick, elderly and widows…were initiated and provided by Christians. Guidelines for safe and healthy living, care for the homeless, sick, elderly and widows…Ten commandments/ belief in God/ Christian holidays…Sundays... no work.

COMMANDMENTS: Basis for the rules of civilization; see Deuteronomy 5.
Laws based on God's Word… basis for rules of civilization to provide for our health and safety. (Even traffic laws e.g. (four way stop…who goes first). Politeness, thoughtfulness.
- Commandments were the basis for our justice system and self-government.
- Manners—How to handle awkward situations (excuse me…thank you!!!, I'm sorry).

GOD'S PLAN FOR FAMILY: *FAMILY SYSTEMS MODEL;* see DEUTERONOMY 5–6.
- Identify how your parents modeled the following patterns in your family.

> Identify your Family's
> **RULES, ROLES, ROUTINES**
> **FAMILY VALUES**

SEE FAMILY SYSTEMS: Diagram 3 generations of your family. Identify how your family functioned and interacted with the world. Make notes of family characteristics; see pg.28.

Homework: Read over material for the next lesson.
COMPLETE: GROUP COUNSELING NOTE to identify what they have learned in this lesson.

THE FAMILY SYSTEMS MODEL

"Wives, submit to your husbands, as is fitting in the Lord. Husbands, love your wives and do not be harsh with them. Children, obey your parents in everything, for this pleases the Lord. Fathers, do not embitter your children, or they will become discouraged." —Colossians 3:18-21

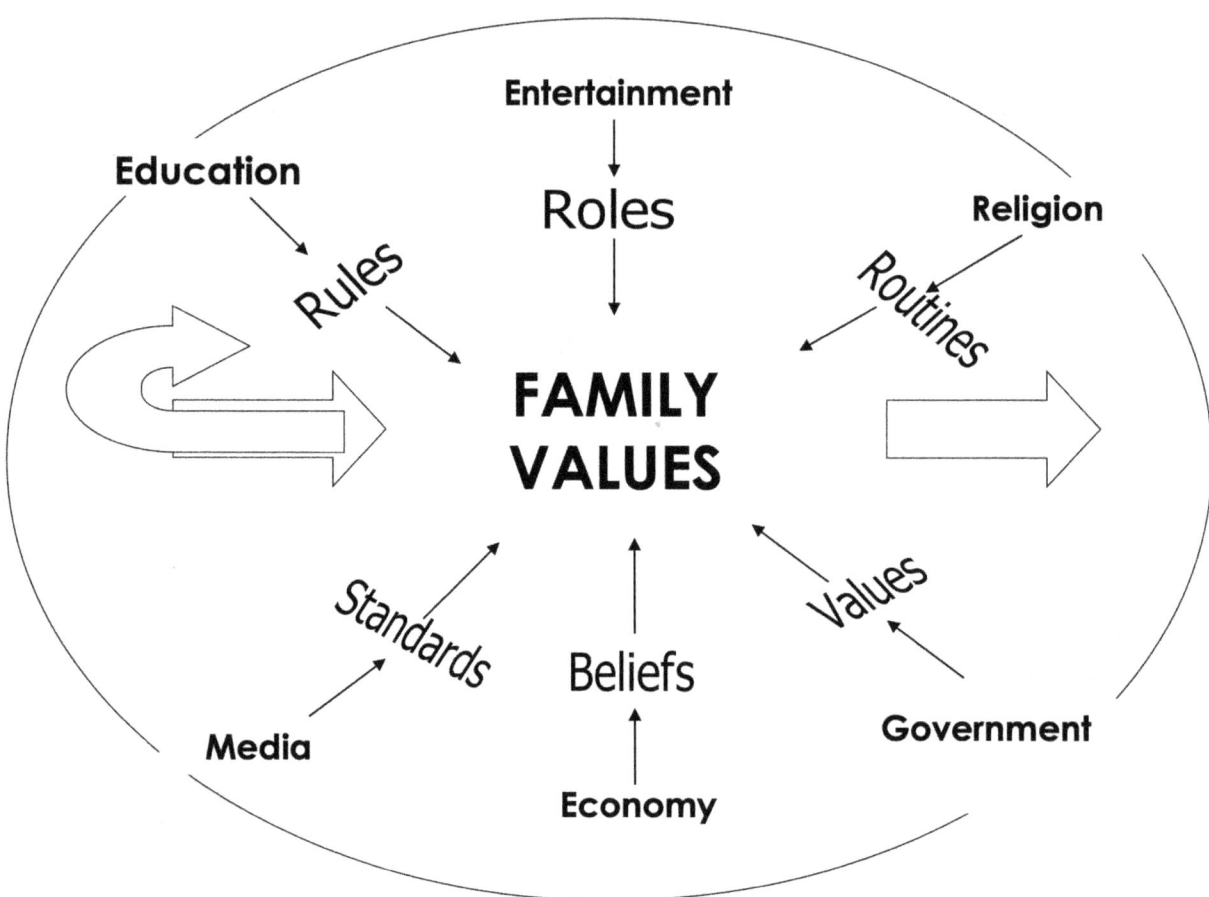

This diagram was from a drawing in my notes from a Personal Growth and Development class led by Proctor & Gamble Co. in the late 60's (best source: The Family Systems Model

LESSON FIVE: FAMILIES MAKE A DIFFERENCE

REVIEW: ANSWERS TO PERSONAL HISTORY QUESTIONNAIRE
- Identify childhood trauma symptoms.
- Identify other trauma producing activities/ events.

INTRODUCTION TO FOUR TYPES OF FAMILIES: *Authoritarian, Chaotic, Rigid, and Showcase*
- Take time to describe each type of family, identifying the roles, rules, rituals, standards, beliefs, and values of each one; see pgs.33–34.

TABLE EXERCISE: Give each table a type of family for which they are to create a skit that would define their specific family type. (5 minutes to plan, 5 minutes to act out). Ask the class to guess family type.

Act out skits…describe the effect of each type of family on the development of children.

Identify the type of family YOU grew up in…
- How did that family style influence the development of your family today?

Describe societal changes: See Statistics—Lesson One
- 1960s–2020: 2 generations of deterioration of marriage, family, health.
- Increase in abortion, suicide, mental health, addictions, pornography, murder.

2020: COVID VIRUS/ SHUTDOWN OF AIRFLIGHT/ SOCIAL DISTANCING/ CLOSING OF BUSINESSES/SCHOOLS/BUSINESSES CLOSED/ WORK, SCHOOL FROM HOME.
SOCIAL WARFARE—MASKS/9 MEDIA/CHURCH/GOVERNMENT/INDUSTRY/MEDICAL

EXERCISE: Note changes that took place in Education, Entertainment, Religion, Media, Economy, and Government in your lifetime. See examples.
- Education: Sex education, no prayer, no Bibles…
- Entertainment—phones, media expansion
- Religion—changes in music, use of media, liberalization of message
- Media—expansion
- Economy
- Government

CYCLE OF DYSFUNCTION: See pg.86.
REFLECTIVE EXERCISE: See pg.36.
BIBLE REFLECTION: Luke 10:19, Ephesians 3:14-19
PRAYER FOR BREAKING CURSES: See pg.36.

Homework: Read over material for the next lesson.
COMPLETE: GROUP COUNSELING NOTE to identify what they have learned in this lesson.

DIAGRAM—*CYCLE OF DYSFUNCTION*: See pg.87.

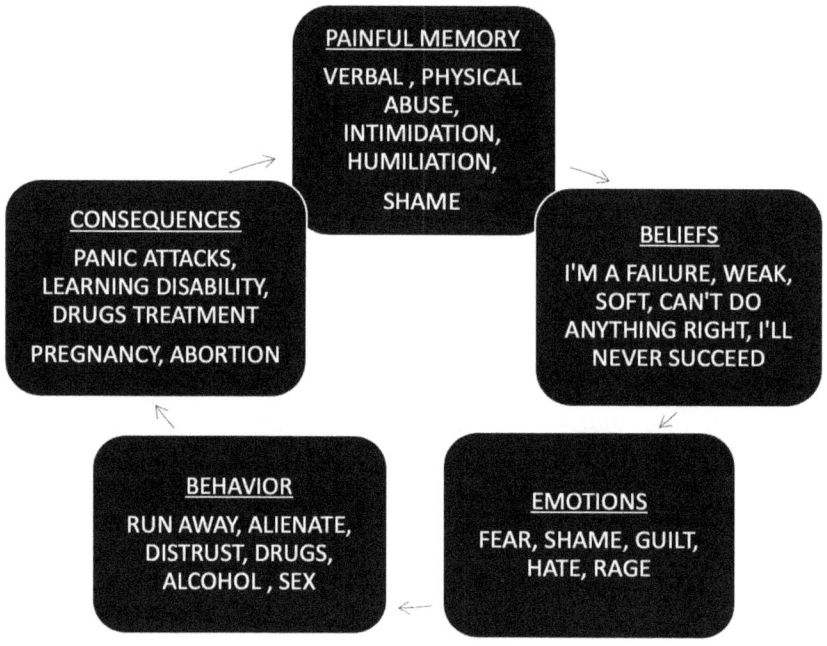

If we have been taught since childhood that we are a child of God who belongs to God's family, God has a purpose for our lives, our name is written in His "Book of Life," God is with us, and He loves us—we will most likely be free to move in our gifting; flowing from developmental stage to developmental stage, without missing a beat. Those who have grown up fearing for their safety and security; believing themselves to be unwanted, unloved, and rejected—often see themselves as "being everybody's problem," "not good enough," and "a failure." Not to mention, their negative life experiences will prove repeatedly that they are unsafe and uncared for. It will be difficult for people who experience this kind of childhood to move freely through the different stages of development because they are experiencing inadequacy, insecurity, failure, etc. These feelings will eventually cause them to develop "defense mechanisms" such as explaining, withdrawing, blaming, procrastination, lying, making excuses, justifying, etc., —they are identifying with their weaknesses, rather than their strengths.

LESSON SIX: GROWING UP IN STAGES:

WE ARE ALL "AGENTS" OF GOD...MADE IN HIS IMAGE...FOR HIS PURPOSE

ICA– Core Self: (revisit) See pg.24.
- Sense of Agency: See pgs.38–40. Take time to explain how the baby gradually learns to understand he is an agent in his world—self, others, surroundings, God (*ICA Theory*).

EXAMINE SELF—MAKE NOTES—SENSE OF AGENCY: Being able to create change; see pg.43.
- Coherency—recognizing he is separate from mother/ has moving parts
- Affectivity—can move parts, touch, feel, move
- Continuity—push legs to move, to climb, to hold objects in hands

BIRTH–12 MONTHS—bonding w/parents (acceptance, worthy of love)
3–9 months—peak of bonding w/parents (acceptance, worthy of love)
2 YEARS—Sensory Tracks—left brain (words & sounds)
  Right brain = voice tone and facial expressions)
3–5 years—Another peak in bonding—by now the child will have attachment to the father.
ADD—ADHD—lack of consistency in rules (separation from M & F) change (babysitters, preschool, Day Care, Boarding School…change of people/ change of rules… etc.)
7–10 years—next peak in bonding
15 years—last major step in bonding—separation begins.
  SENSE OF AGENCY: Feels ready and able to go into the world and make It on his own.

CHILDHOOD TRAUMA: ALCOHOLIC PARENTS, VERBAL, PHYSICAL, SEXUAL ABUSE
Can lead to a spirit of REJECTION, ABANDONMENT, DEATH, SEPARATION, UNLOVED.

REFLECTIVE ACTIVITY: CYCLE OF DYSFUNCTION… See pg.86. **Identify** how thoughts and perceptions connect with emotions, and lead to actions often based on lies/misperceptions because as children, we do not have ALL the information to base our decisions on.

PRAYER FOR HEALING OF DEVELOPMENTAL SCARS FAMILY PURPOSE: See pg.44.

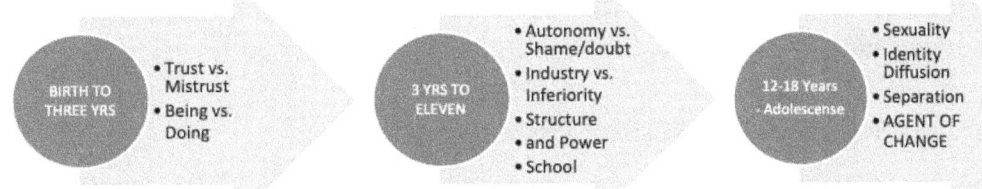

HOMEWORK: IDENTIFY TRAUMA'S EFFECT OF DEVELOPMENT AND HOW YOUR LIFE EXPERIENCES AFFECT YOUR VIEW OF SELF/ OTHERS/WORLD AND God. See pg.41.
…identify any DEVELOPMENTAL SCARS DUE TO LACK OF BONDING …shame, guilt, abuse…just for being YOU. **BELIEF**: "no one is going to care for me…I must take care of myself." Read over material for the next lesson.
COMPLETE: GROUP COUNSELING NOTE to identify what they have learned in this lesson.

SENSE OF AGENCY

MASTERING LIFE…. LEARNING SELF CARE
Learning to nurse/suck from a bottle
Learn to feed self
Holding a spoon/ pencil
Crawl, stand, walk, run
Climbing stairs

DIFFERENT STAGES OF GROWTH FOR EACH AGE GROUP…. (See Developmental Stages)
If we have been taught since childhood that we are a child of God who belongs to God's family, God has a purpose for our lives, our name is written in His "Book of Life," God is with us, and He loves us—we will most likely be free to move in our gifting; flowing from developmental stage to developmental stage, without missing a beat. Those who have grown up fearing for their safety and security; believing themselves to be unwanted, unloved, and rejected—often see themselves as "being everybody's problem," "not good enough," and "a failure." Not to mention, their negative life experiences will prove repeatedly that they are unsafe and uncared for. It will be difficult for people who experience this kind of childhood to move freely through the different stages of development because they are experiencing inadequacy, insecurity, failure, etc. These feelings will eventually cause them to develop "defense mechanisms" such as explaining, withdrawing, blaming, procrastination, lying, making excuses, justifying, etc., —they are identifying with their weaknesses, rather than their strengths.

PRAYER for HEALING SCARS/FAULTY BELIEFS: See pg.44.

Homework: Read over material for the next lesson.
COMPLETE: GROUP COUNSELING NOTE to identify what they have learned in this lesson.

LESSON SEVEN: TAKING THE AX TO THE ROOT

Get feedback from the Developmental Stages—How did you see your childhood issues playing a part in your daily life today? (Where did you get stuck?)

Jewish people –Slaves in Egypt experienced hunger & drought in their land…Joseph's family settled in Egypt where there was food…430 years…then God helped then escape from slavery—They had a **SLAVE IMAGE**… No value/worth, dependent on others, slaves, no power; **NOW**, with God's help—solid ground to stand on… Ten Commandments…God's love and sovereign care for His people. However, while Moses was on the mountain getting the Ten Commandments, they rebelled—worshipped other gods…idols…took gold and made a golden calf (idol).
- See Blessings and Curses: See pg.47; Deut. 5: 9-10.
- REFLECTIVE EXERCISE: See pg.48.

PRAYER FOR BREAKING GENERATIONAL CURSES: See pg.49.

IDENTIFY ROOTS OF BITTERNESS…TAKE THE AX TO THE ROOT: See Biblical Reflections on pg.50.

EXPLAIN GENOGRAM: See pgs.50–51.
- Diagram three generations of family.
- HOW TO USE THE GENOGRAM; see pgs.51–56. (see sample copy—next page, May be used to make copies).
- IDENTIFY THREE GENERATIONS OF YOUR FAMILY HISTORY (family "roots").

ROOTS OF BITTERNESS: Story of the Prodigal son; see pg.49… bitterness, jealousy, Jacob & Esau. (60s movie "ROOTS"—slaves in America—looking for their roots—relate to today's abuse, human trafficking…mental/physical/psychological slavery….).
- Identify ROOT CAUSES OF PROBLEMS IN FAMILY; see pg.48.
- Blessings & Curses; see pg.47.

REFLECTIVE EXERCISE: See pg.48.

TODAY'S FALSE GODS: (Slaves to idols/gods)—Identify how one becomes a "worshipper of 'false gods". DRUGS, ALCOHOL, MONEY, POWER, CONTROL, SEX, FOOD, PORNOGRAPHY SOCIAL MEDIA—TELEPHONES, NEWS, WELFARE, TV. SPORTS.

IDENTIFY BLESSINGS/CURSES OVER YOUR LIFE/FAMILY: See pgs.47–48.
WHY PEOPLE SUFFER CURSES: THIRD AND FOURTH GENERATIONS—IDENTIFY EXAMPLES.
Using the above tools as well as your Personal Questionnaire—Identify Strongholds.

PRAYER: BREAKING GENERATIONAL CURSES; see pg.49. **Add information to your Genogram:** See pg.52.

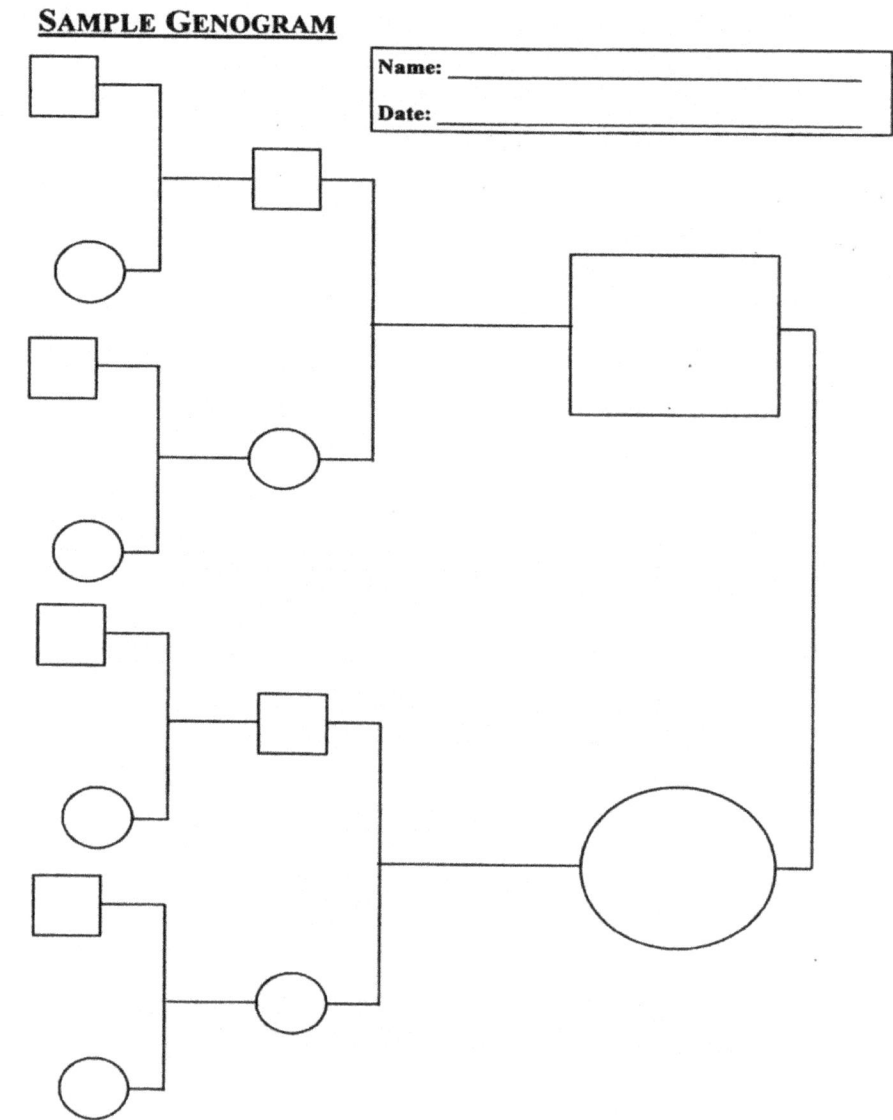

LESSON EIGHT: WALLS WE BUILD

REVIEW information on *Personal Inventory & Genogram*
- We have explored the Blessings and Curses, Family Systems, ICA, Tree of Freedom & Tree of Bondage, Developmental Stages and Taking the Ax to the Root…
- We have also pulled down strongholds of generational curses and strongholds.

TODAY WE'RE GOING TO LOOK AT walls we build (Isaiah 25:12, Proverbs 14:12).
Adam and Eve…experienced. Shame & guilt after they disobeyed God…. BUILT WALLS OF FEAR OF DISAPPROVAL—hid behind fig leaves—(defense. Cover-up shame/guilt). Read Genesis 3:6-7.
"HE (God) must increase, and I must decrease" … (Wanting to be our own God, or realizing HE is greater and has a plan for our lives) …therefore, HE can guide us, teach us, protect us, and lead us in the plan He has for us). —John 3:30

DEFENSE MECHANISMS: Child's efforts to solve problem based on his/her perception; see pgs.39, 40,41.—(often find ways of saving face or desiring to please others to protect self) e.g., empty arguments (excuses/ defenses).

DEMONSTRATE: How we build walls of protection from shame and guilt.

EXERCISE: Common Defense Mechanisms
- **TABLE ACTIVITY**: Identify all the defense mechanisms you have used in your daily life and why! See pgs.61—64.

GIVE EACH PERSON A BRICK/ STICKY NOTES:
- Ask each person to identify what defense mechanisms they recognize in their own life, and why they think they use these particular defense mechanisms.
- COME FORWARD TO SHARE THEIR BRICK…BUILD WALL.
    - Confession: 1 COR. 4: 7-12
    - Dying to Self: Romans 15:13
    - PRAYER TO BREAK POWER OF LIES: See pg.66.

Homework: Identify faulty beliefs you desire to lay down/ give to Jesus. Read over material for the next lesson.
COMPLETE: GROUP COUNSELING NOTE to identify what they have learned in this lesson.

DEFENSE MECHANISMS

Identify defense mechanisms (lies you believed) you have used as a child, youth and now as an adult: See the entire list of *DEFENSE MECHANISMS* on pgs.61–64 in the PHH Student Book.

<u>Blaming</u>: "It's all his fault."
<u>The Lie:</u> "Mistakes or accidents are not tolerated; I must not let them know I did this."

<u>People Pleasing</u>: "Sure, I can lend you $500."
<u>The Lie:</u> "I must do whatever you want me to do to get you to like me."

<u>Lying:</u> "I didn't hear him say anything."
<u>The Lie:</u> "If I tell the truth, I'll make him hate me. I couldn't stand that."

<u>Rationalizing</u>: "Aw, I did okay. Everybody got bad grades. Only the teacher's pets passed."
<u>The Lie:</u> "I can't tell anyone I failed. It would be too shameful."

<u>Withdrawal</u>: "I'm not feeling well, so I'm not going to the party."
<u>The Lie:</u> "I can't face those people because they'll think I'm fat and ugly."

<u>Acquiescing</u>: "Yeah, I guess I could go, if my Mom and Dad will let me."
<u>The Lie:</u> "I don't have the right to say "no."

<u>Attacking</u>: "I'll bust you in the nose if you come close."
<u>The Lie:</u> "I can't trust anyone, so I won't let you get close to me. You'll hurt me like all the others."

<u>Getting High</u>: "I can't handle this anymore. I need a drink."
<u>The Lie:</u> "I am more effective after a drink (or a joint, etc.)."

<u>Put Downs</u>: "Oh, you're so stupid. Who's going to listen to you!"
<u>The Lie:</u> "If I put you down, it will make me feel more important."

LESSON NINE: WEB OF LIES

BIBLICAL PRINCIPLE: SOWING AND REAPING
- Matthew 12:33
- Galatians 6:7-9
- Proverbs 19:5
- Hosea 10:12

REFLECTION:
- Put in your own words the concept of sowing and reaping....
- Identify experiences you have had regarding sowing and reaping in your personal life.
    - How did your experience relate to the experience Eve had in the Garden when she ate the forbidden fruit?

Note: Eve was ashamed and embarrassed when blamed by the serpent! Adam who also partook felt guilty.... both covered themselves with grape Leaves to cover their shame.

ALTERNATIVES, CHOICES, TEMPTATIONS are all part of life. **TEMPTATIONS LIKE ..."** If it feels good, do it!!!!". "One time won't hurt!!" "Everybody else is doing it!"
- WHAT DOES THIS SAY ABOUT THE IMPORTANCE OF **KNOWING THE "TRUTH"** ...
- Or...WHAT DOES THIS SAY ABOUT **NOT OBEYING RULES**???
    - HOW DO WE KNOW WHAT GOD'S WILL IS?
    - HOW DO WE AVOID BEING TEMPTED? LIED TO? BULLIED INTO?
    - FALLING PREY?

TABLE ACTIVITY—TYPES OF LIES WE BELIEVE: Complete the Reflective Exercise; see pgs.69–70.

SCHEMATIZATION—SCHEMA ... GOD'S PERCEPTION Vs. MY PERCEPTION: See pg.72. "Mental Picture with all the emotions involved, perceptions... (EVERYBODY, NOBODY, ALWAYS, NEVER)
- Identify one memory that you recognize your body has a fine-tuned SCHEMATIZATION or SCHEMA.
- Discuss this at the home table.
- Complete reflection on pgs.70–71.

EXAMPLE: You see just ahead of you what looks like a black snake on the path ahead of you. Your heart begins to beat fast, and it pounds against your chest...you remember that snakes are poisonous, but also can attack and bite you. Your brain is connecting with your mental and neurological perceptions, and your body is reacting to the picture in your mind. As you get closer, you realize it is just a dead stick lying on the path and you pick it up and toss it away!!!!
- What does this say about "perception"? Schematization?

GOD'S PERCEPTION/ MY PERCEPTION:
- Identify your "Schema"
- Compare "my" truth to GOD'S TRUTH
- Read and remember scriptures to replace the lies you believe…. this is called RENEWING THE MIND WITH THE WORD OF GOD! See pg.72.

Identify memories that hold lies: See pg.73.
- Read list of Satan's lies he tricks people into believing
- Identify the lies you have been believing
- Renew your mind with the Word of truth

Homework: Read over material for the next lesson.
COMPLETE: GROUP COUNSELING NOTE to identify what they have learned in this lesson.

GATE-CONTROL THEORY: How the brain can modify the feeling of pain and symptoms

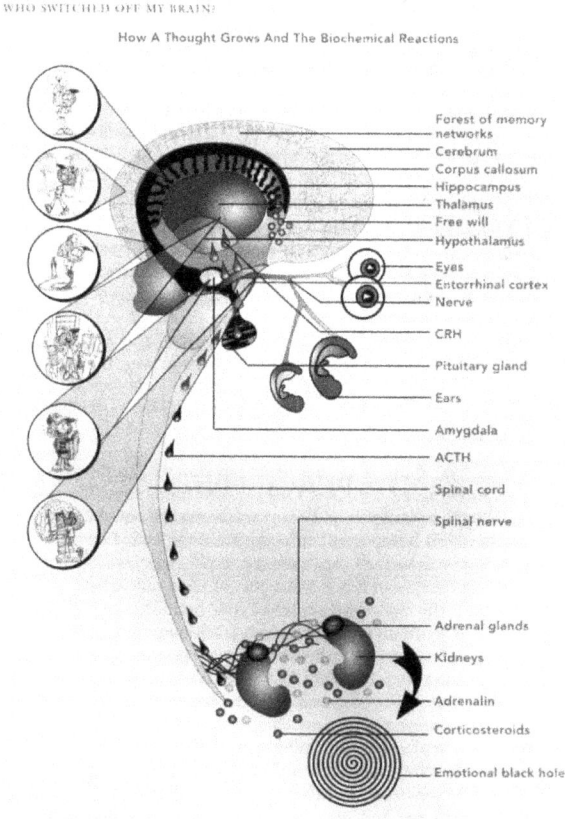

Resource: *Who Switched Off My Brain*, by Caroline Leaf

LESSON TEN: LIES, OATHS, AND VOWS

SHARE (READ) CARRIE'S STORY that helped her mother to "IDENTIFY WHAT CAUSED CARRIES DETOUR THAT LED TO DRUG USE AND REHABILITATION." See pg.75.
- *"For God, who commanded the light to shine out of darkness, hath shined in our hearts, to give the light of the knowledge of the glory of God in the face of Jesus Christ."* —II Corinthians 4:6
- Read Isaiah 28:15
- Read Psalms 120:2

MEMORIES EMBEDDED IN THE WOUND.... Hold **TRUTH**, but they also hold lies.
HIPPOCAMPUS: If we are going to be able to move beyond our past negative experiences, we must recognize that our brains are created in such a way that they can be renewed. *There is a tie between the Hippocampus and our thoughts, feelings, and behavior. It is the hippocampus that holds the thoughts until we decide that they are insignificant and should be released or stored.* See pgs.75–76.

OATHS AND VOWS…WORDS SPOKEN OVER US: See pg.79.
- Proverbs 20:25
- Isaiah 28:15
- Psalms 120:2

RENOUNCING OATHS AND VOWS… PROMISES WE MAKE TO OURSELVES: See pg.77.
- James 3:4-10
- Hosea 10:4
- Matthew 5:33

THE POWER OF THE TONGUE Scriptures: See pgs.76–77.
OATHS AND VOWS WE SPEAK OVER OTHERS: See pg.77.
- Power of the tongue—James 3: 4-6, 3:10
- "Out of the overflow of the heart the mouth speaks."—Matthew 12:34

INNER VOWS—PROMISES WE MAKE TO OURSELVES: Examples on pg.78.
- Psalm 51—God honors a broken and contrite heart. a heart full of compassion and teachable
- Job 22-27
- Psalm 51:6
- Isaiah 19:21
- Proverbs 20:25

RENOUNCING OATHS AND VOWS: Sample prayer on pg.81.

Homework: Continue praying and releasing oaths and vows. Read over material for the next lesson.
COMPLETE: GROUP COUNSELING NOTE to identify what they have learned in this lesson.

LESSON ELEVEN: OUT OF DARKNESS

JO-HARI WINDOW: The Public Self, My Blind Spots, My Hidden Self, My unconscious Self
- Define each (methods used to survive pain). See chart on pg.83.

IMPRINTS: Dominant imprints come from parents (we do what they model).
- Fearful imprints that program us for future fearful thought patterns and behaviors
- Fear of certain subjects or objects—an example of bad experience generating generalized fear
- (Use example of being bit by a dog.) When an incident is repeated it creates a distinctive pattern of neuron activity

FEARS ARE LODGED IN THE HIPPOCAMPUS (part of the brain that holds memories.) This is why fears stay with us and hinder us from moving forward in our growth. See pgs.84, 90.

YOUR MEMORY AND HOW IT WORKS: See diagram on pg.84.

BOOK: Who Switched Off My Brain by Dr. Caroline Leaf
- **Pre-frontal Cortex: T**akes seven repetitions to get from short to long term memory. See pg.84.
- **Hippocampus:** Long-term memory (the stronger the emotion, the easier it is to remember). See pg.84.
- **Limbic System**—Everything passes through and is given emotional value.—(Fight or Flight); See pg.75.

EMOTIONS are often a clue to what is hidden within; things we have feared to remember or discuss. See pg.76.
CYCLE OF DYSFUNCTION: Dan's Story diagrammed; See pg.87.
DEFENSE MECHANISMS: Dan's Story; See pg.89.
SEE LIST OF DEFENSE MECHANISMS: Disempowered; See pgs.61–64.
CYCLE OF ILLUMINATION: See pg.91.
IDENTIFY STEPS OF ILLUMINATION: See pg.91.
- Childhood memory (perception, emotions)
- Seek to identify root of emotions/perceptions = Action
- Memories reveal lies.
- Ask God to reveal the truth.
- God reveals truth.
- Release—broken bondage

> *Only when we are aware of our thoughts, feelings, can we express them out loud, and have a voice. If we don't have a voice, how will we be able to fulfill our life. purpose?*

*"Search me, O God, and know my heart: try me, and know my thoughts:
And see if there be any wicked way in me and lead me in the way everlasting."* —Psalm 139:23-24

JOHARI WINDOW

	Known to Self	Unknown to Self
Known to Others	My Public Self	My Blind Spot
Unknown to Others	My Hidden Self	My Unconscious Self

The Johari Window, named for its creators—Joseph Luft and Harry Ingham

- Reflect on your awareness of your "Public Self", your "Blind Spots", your "Hidden Self and your Unconscious Self.

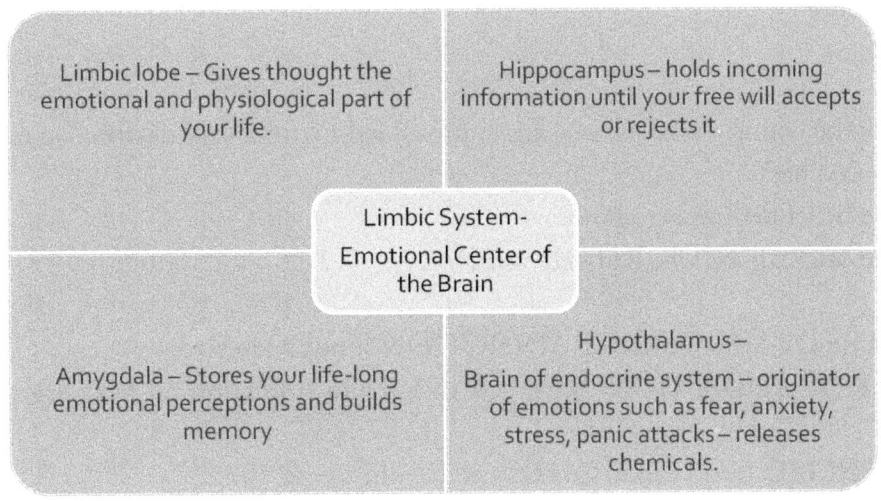

Homework: Read over material for the next lesson.
COMPLETE: GROUP COUNSELING NOTE to identify what they have learned in this lesson.

LESSON TWELVE: CYCLE OF SIN AND ADDICTION/ ICEBERG THEORY

"SEEING THE TIP OF THE ICEBERG"

NON-VERBAL—WORDS, TONE OF VOICE, BODY LANGUAGE AND GESTURES REVEAL WHAT IS GOING ON INSIDE YOUR MIND/BODY
- LOOK WITHIN TO SEE THE DEEPER STRUCTURE OF YOUR THOUGHTS; pgs.95–96.
- Tell story of male student who scrawled across the school chalk board with lipstick: **I HATE YOU ALL!** pgs.95–96. TIP OF THE ICEBERG……WHAT EVERYONE SEES!

READ STORY OF YOUNG WOMAN ON NEW JOB WHO WAS HAVING DIFFICULTY WITH HER BOSS.
- Identify the THREE underlying causes of her feelings/actions.
- What was the TIP OF THE ICEBERG?
- What was "beneath the water"?
- What was the "truth" that set her free?
- Was the "hidden" lie?

Biblical Reflections:
CYCLE OF SIN AND ADDICTION: See pgs.97–98.
- Identify the "Terms"

REFLECTION:
- Describe how the young woman's need for approval led her to a very destructive relationship with a male who abused her?
- What was the belief behind her choice?
- What was the original "lie" she had believed???

Identify how CYCLES OF SIN can lead to ADDICTION if not addressed.
REFER TO CYCLE OF ADDICTION: See Cycle of Sin and Addiction on next page; also see workbook pg.98.
REFLECTIVE EXERCISE: Sins Lead to Sickness & Death; see pg.102.
BIBLICAL REFLECTIONS: Hebrews 4:13, Psalm 33:18, Zechariah 8:16
SIN LEADS TO SICKNESS AND DEATH: Identify causes. See pg.101. See Hebrews 3:7-8:12.

Generational patterns of self-protection and survival:
- Long term habitual sin (stress, worry, anxiety, fear, anger, resentment…)
- Unforgiven transgressions
- Emotional turmoil (anger/hate/ lack of sleep, nightmares…)

REFLECTIVE EXERCISE: See pg.102.
Add to GENOGRAM: See pg.52.
PRAYER TO BREAK BONDAGES: See pg.49.

Homework: Read over material for the next lesson.
COMPLETE: GROUP COUNSELING NOTE to identify what they have learned in this lesson.

CYCLE OF SIN AND ADDICTION

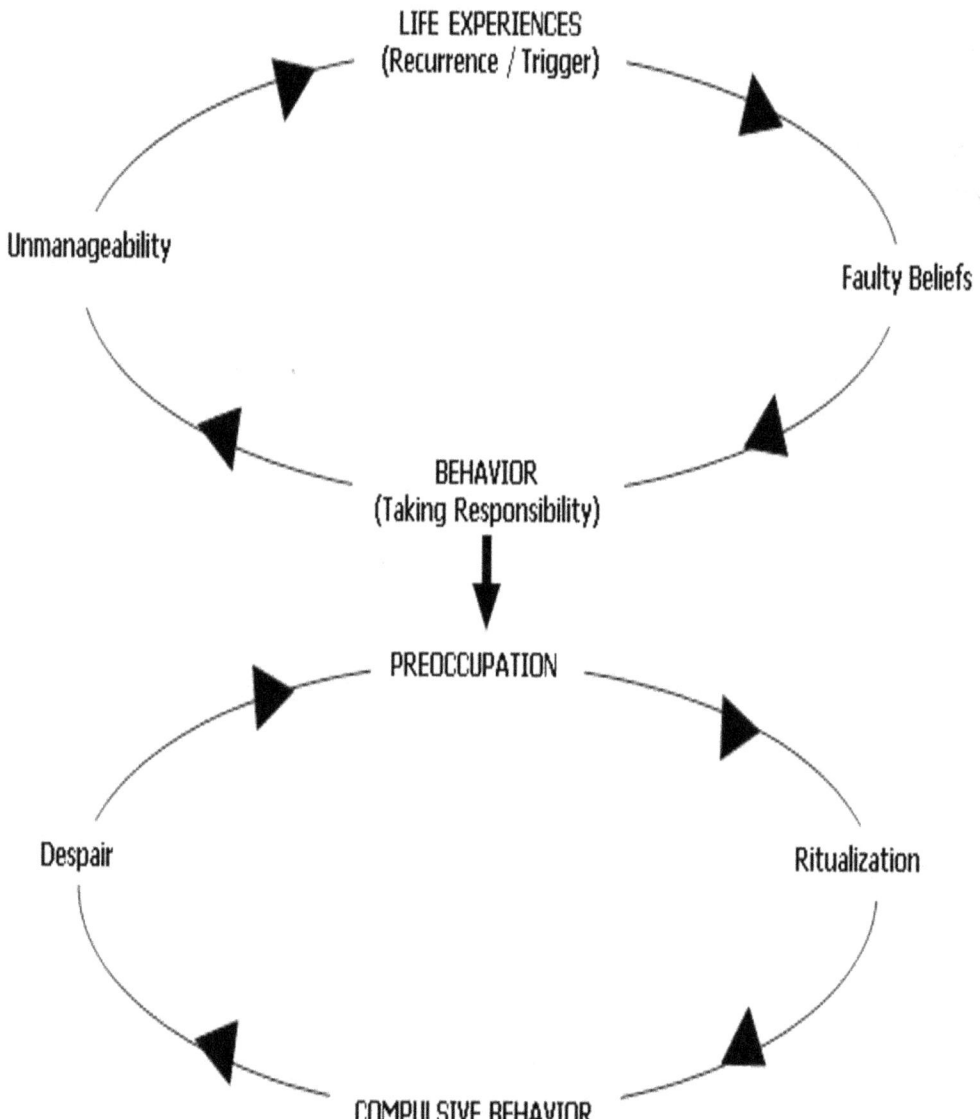

LESSON THIRTEEN: HEALTHY BOUNDARIES

"In the day that thy walls are to be built, in that day shall the decree be far removed." —Micah 7:11

- What are boundaries? Purpose? See pg.104.

Changing unhealthy patterns of family interaction; See pg.105. See 1Timothy 3:5.

FENCES KEEP BAD THINGS OUT.

Setting healthy boundaries for children. Healthy families put healthy **boundaries** in place to protect the child from danger. Different kinds of **boundaries**... directions, correction, teaching, instruction, discipline; see pgs.104–105. —Ephesians 4:22-5:2

SEE "LOVING WAYS TO CREATE SAFE RELATIONSHIPS"—CHANGE UNHEALTHY PATTERNS OF FAMILY INTERACTION: See pg.105.

"For if a man know not how to rule his own house, how shall he take care of the church of God?" —1 Timothy 3:5

HOW GOD CHANGES US: David...the shepherd boy, Zaccheus the tax collector; See pg.105.
INSTRUCTIONS TO THE EPHESIANS: See pg.106. See Ps. 34:4.

BIBLICAL REFLECTIONS: See 1Timothy 5:4, Colossians 3:8.
REFLECTIVE EXERCISE: Changing unhealthy patterns of family interaction; See pg.105.

SETTING HEALTHY BOUNDARIES—FREE FROM FEAR: See pgs.105, 107.
- SAFE AND UNSAFE PLACES
- QUALITIES OF SAFE PLACES
- QUALITIES OF UNSAFE PLACES

REFLECTIVE TABLE EXERCISES: Answer the questions regarding your environment. See pg.109.
PRAYER TO CHANGE UNHEALTHY FAMILY RELATIONSHIPS: See pg.109.

IDENTIFY WAYS TO CREATE SAFE BOUNDARIES:
- Teach, uphold, and practice God's laws.
- Love according to I Corinthians 13
- Help people consider the consequences of their words and actions.
- Help people identify the lies of the enemy.
- Practice praying and confessing the Word.
- Teach and model repentance and forgiveness.
- Model and teach humble confessions of sins.
- Provide an atmosphere of caring and compassion.
- Pray with one another.
- Confess God's promises over each other.
- Practice the fruits of the Spirit: love, joy, peace, patience, kindness, goodness, faithfulness, gentleness, and self-control.
- Read the Word aloud in every room of your house.

PRAYER TO CHANGE UNHEALTHY FAMILY RELATIONSHIPS: See pg.109.
God's Words set boundaries for our lives. On pg.106 of the Student Book you will find Ephesians 4:22—5:2…Read this section and identify BOUNDARIES God has set up for us through His Word.

_____
_____
_____
_____

Homework: Read over material for the next lesson.
COMPLETE: GROUP COUNSELING NOTE to identify what they have learned in this lesson.

LESSON FOURTEEN: BREAKING FREE

GUIDE TO SPIRITUAL SURGERY: See pgs.111–112.

"Behold, I will bring it health and cure, and I will cure them, and will reveal unto them the abundance of peace and truth." —Jeremiah 33:6

> **BAND-AIDS DON'T HEAL WOUNDS...**

- Identify Qualities of SAFE PLACES as opposed to UNSAFE PLACES. See pgs.107–108.
- Identify your SAFE PLACE while growing up!!!

STAGES OF THE HEALING PROCESS: Review of Learnings; see pgs.124–125.
- Tree of Freedom/ Tree of Bondage
- Generational Patterns—Genogram
- Underlying beliefs—Developmental Scars, Personal Inventory Questionnaire
- Life patterns—Defense Mechanisms
- View of self/life—My Perception/ God's Perception

FASTING: See pg.113.
- Plea for deliverance: *"Is not this the fast that I have chosen? to loose the bands of wickedness, to undo the heavy burdens, and to let the oppressed go free, and that ye break every yoke? Is it not to deal thy bread to the hungry, and that thou bring the poor that are cast out to thy house? when thou seest the naked, that thou cover him; and that thou hide not thyself from thine own flesh?"* Isaiah 58: 6-7
- for nation's sins: Daniel 9:19
- personal sins: Matthew 6:16
- demonic activity: Matthew 17:21
- principalities: Ephesians 6:10-17

REPENTANCE: See pgs.114–115.
- Healing Power of Repentance: Acts 17:30

BIBLICAL REFLECTION & REFLECTIVE EXERCISE: See pgs.117–118.
SAMPLE PRAYER OF FORGIVENESS: See pg.119.

RENOUNCING TIES TO CULTS, OCCULT, AND WITCHCRAFT:
- *"Regard not them that have familiar spirits, neither seek after wizards, to be defiled by them: I am the Lord your God."* —Leviticus 19:31
- *"Associate yourselves, O ye people, and ye shall be broken in pieces; and give ear, all ye of far countries: gird yourselves, and ye shall be broken in pieces; gird yourselves, and ye shall be broken in pieces."* —Isaiah 8:19

- *"Moreover the workers with familiar spirits, and the wizards, and the images, and the idols, and all the abominations that were spied in the land of Judah and in Jerusalem, did Josiah put away, that he might perform the words of the law which were written in the book that Hilkiah the priest found in the house of the LORD."* —2Kings 23:24

STEPS TO FORGIVENESS: See pgs.116–117. See Psalms 32:1-2.

Steps of Forgiveness:

1. Line your will up with God's will. Purpose in your heart to work the process through — regardless of the pain and fear.
2. Ask the Holy Spirit to shed His light into your soul to reveal the roots of the bitterness in your heart.
3. Be specific about what it is you need to forgive.
4. Identify your response to the offense.
5. Be honest before God regarding how you feel about the person or the event.
6. Forgive the offense.
7. Pray and ask God to forgive you for holding the unforgiveness in your heart.
8. Identify any inner vows you have made regarding your offender and renounce them.
9. Renew your mind with the Word of God.
10. Forgive yourself for your part and pray for healing.
11. Identify any area in which you are blaming God.
12. Release God, others, and yourself from any false or unrealistic expectations you may have had for them.
13. Forgive God. Ask Him to show you what He was trying to work into your spirit.
14. Prayer for the person you have forgiven.

Standing on the Promises: See pgs.72,120.
REFLECTIVE EXERCISE: See pg.115.
PRAYER TO RENOUNCE CULT AND OCCULT INVOLVEMENT: See pg.121.

Homework: Read over material for the next lesson.
Complete: Group Counseling Note to identify what they have learned in this session.

LESSON FIFTEEN: RENEWING THE MIND

"And be not conformed to this world: but be ye transformed by the renewing of your mind, that ye may prove what is that good, and acceptable, and perfect, will of God." —Romans 12:2

MIND—PLAYGROUND OF THE ENEMY: See Romans 8:1-2.

WHAT MIND RENEWAL IS NOT: See pg.123.
- Changing the memory or removing the memory but ...rather reinterpretation of the memory by replacing the embedded lie with the truth.
- Shame and guilt are merely the emotions that match the belief we embrace.

WHAT MIND RENEWAL IS: See pg.124.

EMBRACING TRUTH: Lies can keep us from the ability or desire to grasp or logically agree with the truth. God will reveal the source of that pain as well as the accompanying lie(s). Once we hear the truth from God, it empowers us to move on with our lives. See pg.124.
- Galatians 5:1
- II Corinthians 10:3-4
- John 8:31-32
- Hebrews 9:14
- 1 Peter 5:8-9

REFLECTIVE EXERCISES:
- Renewing the mind: See pg.125.
- Power of lies: See pgs.125–126.

REFLECTIVE EXERCISE:
- Steps to Renewing the Mind—conduct at table; see pgs.125–126.

DYING TO SELF: See pgs.128–129.
Defense Mechanisms: See pgs.61–64.
- Galatians 5:1
- Matthew 24:12—
- STORY OF LAZARUS—John 11: 41-44 (skit)

SKIT: See next page.
- From bondage to freedom: See pg.133.

REFLECTIONS: Dying to Self; see pg.133.
Prayer for Dying to Self: See pg.129.

- Transformation: See pgs.127,129.
- Restoring Your Sense of Identity: See pgs.129–130.

Self-Study: Who Am I In Christ? See pg.130.
Changing Faulty Beliefs: See pgs.130–131.

> **Find a safe place to practice your new behavior! pg. 131**

REFLECTIVE EXERCISE:
- Take time to identify faulty beliefs & behavioral problems, then pray for protection from the enemy, and for healing and restoration. See pgs.130–134.

ROLEPLAY: Lazarus died, and Jesus called him from the grave; read John 11:38.
Lazarus was wrapped in grave clothes. He had been dead for four days and the body would have begun to decay. Jesus said to those watching: "Take off the grave cloths and let him go."
As you unwrap the grave clothes, his body comes to life...His brain switches on, uncover his eyes, he sees again...when you uncover his nose, he breaths again, his mouth, he begins to speak...his hand/ arms, he begins to reach out to others...then his heart is set free. Then his body and legs and he is a free man...the grave clothes have been removed and he has been given NEW LIFE. Such is the salvation of every soul God speaks His life into.

Lazarus wrapped in toilet paper or gauze...............

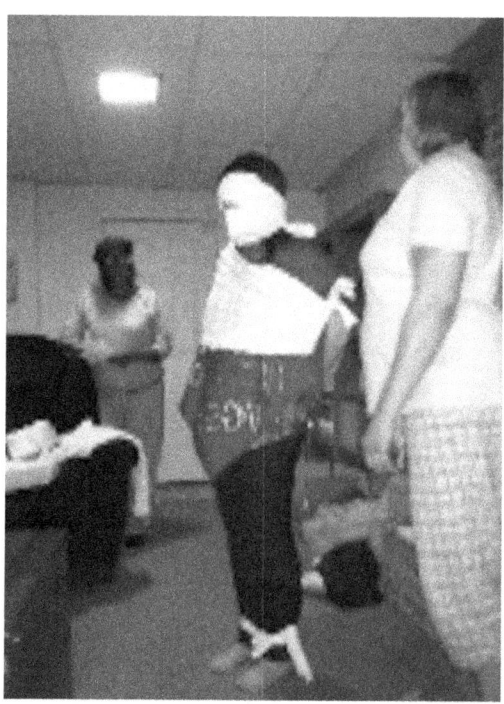

Complete: Group Counseling Note to identify what they have learned in this session. What is the group counseling note.

CLOSING EXERCISE:

1. Each person is given back their brick with their list of defense mechanisms on it. They are to stand one at a time to identify who they are and their defense mechanism…and describe the walls they built to protect self.
2. They are to take their brick, lay it on the floor in front of the cross…paving a pathway to the Cross. As they lay their brick down…it is laying their defenses down (lies they believed) and pray for God to replace them with healthy boundaries.
3. Once every person has presented their bricks, the group will come together, and the closing exercise will take place:
4. Read Isaiah 61:1-4.
5. Names of graduates will be called and Certificates with their name will be given to them.
6. Close with prayer and dedication of each participant.

Lay down your defense mechanisms:
…. let your walls become paths to the cross/Salvation.

"CLASS BLESSING"

Everyone will get maximum benefit from this class as we learn to bless one another by following these simple rules.

- TURN OFF CELL PHONES.
- Be on time.
- Respect group activity time limits. *Make sure your partners get equal time.*
- Ask questions. Remember: *No question is a "DUMB" question.*
- Participate freely in the discussion.
- Respect the views and perspectives of others though different from yours.
- Do your homework.

REMEMBER, WE ARE A WORK IN PROGRESS!

PERSONAL INVENTORY QUESTIONNAIRE

In order to look more closely at our families and develop our *genogram*, a tool used to identify patterns (positive and/or negative) that may have been passed down from generation to generation, this questionnaire is helpful as a probe into the past and an examination of your current life status in multiple areas. Many people have forgotten some of the details of their growing-up years—this tool asks probing questions to help you remember things you may have forgotten over time. It is also quite useful for anyone in the helping profession who has been or could be helpful to you in this journey. It provides an overall picture of who you are and where you have come from in a relatively short amount of time.

Name _____

Age _____   Sex _____ M _____ F   Birthplace _____

Current marital status _____

Education (highest grade completed) _____ Grade school _____ High School _____ Years of College _____ Other

Are you currently employed and/or going to school? If so, where? _____

List anything significant about your current or past work or school experience.
_____
_____
_____

FAMILY HISTORY

Were you raised by anyone other than your parents? _____

If so, explain _____

Are you adopted? _____

How many children are in your childhood family? _____

Where are you in your family line of siblings? _____

Relationship to father during childhood   GOOD   BAD   INDIFFERENT
Relationship to mother during childhood   GOOD   BAD   INDIFFERENT
Relationship to siblings during childhood   GOOD   BAD   INDIFFERENT

Has there been significant change in any of these relationships? Please explain.

Father	Living	Deceased	Unknown
Mother	Living	Deceased	Unknown
Sibling	Living	Deceased	Unknown
Sibling	Living	Deceased	Unknown
Sibling	Living	Deceased	Unknown
Sibling	Living	Deceased	Unknown

Broken home   Removed from home   Unhappy childhood
Loneliness   Excessive fear   Night terrors
Stammering   Bed wetting   Nail biting
Sleep walking   Physical disabilities   Learning disabilities
Other learning problems

____Molestation   ____Sexual encounters   ____Incest
____Frequent illnesses   ____Serious illnesses

Parent's Remarriage: Please explain any important information regarding your parent's marital history.

Parents Marital Status: Married... How many years _____ Separated...How old were you? _____
Divorced...How old were you? _____ Never Married _____ Widowed
Relationship: Good / Bad / Indifferent

Parents Religious Background:
Father _____
Mother _____
Stepparents _____

General health of your parents and siblings growing up and currently.

Did your parents wish you were of the opposite sex?
In your opinion, did your parents wish you had never been born? How many children do you have?
Ages and Names _____

What is your current relationship with your children?
_____

With whom are you now living? _____

Does your name have any particular significance as to family tradition or cultural or national heritage?
_____

What nationality or cultural/ethic group do you most identify with?
_____

What was the work and economic status of your family growing up?
_____

example: *blue collar family living paycheck to paycheck, unemployed at poverty level, financially secure and middle to upper class status, etc.*

Identify where your parents and siblings fit in relationship to the love you feel FROM and FOR them—how close or far away were they to you while growing up? Place them on this chart where you would place them relative to how close you felt to them or how closely they related to you.

Think about your family and friends. Identify how you feel when you are around them. Circle your answer.

INCLUDED vs. EXCLUDED
VISIBLE AND NEEDED vs. INVISIBLE AND INADEQUATE
FREE TO EXPRESS FEELINGS AND IDEAS or HINDERED
LIKE A LEADER vs. A FOLLOWER
LIFE OF THE PARTY vs. PARTY POOPER
LOVED AND ACCEPTED vs. UNLOVED AND UNACCEPTED
FEELING OF BELONGING vs. AN OUTSIDER

RELIGIOUS AND SPIRITUAL HISTORY

Church Affiliation: Present/Past
_____

Are you a born-again believer? _____   When were you saved? _____
Water Baptized? _____   If so, what age? _____
How often do you currently attend church? _____

Do you have regular devotions in the Bible? _____
Do you find prayer difficult? _____
Have there been any contacts or involvement in your personal life or family history with areas such as occults, middle eastern or new age religions, paganism, consulting with mediums or psychics, tarot card, palm, or horoscope readings, conjuring of spirits, black or white magic or any other activity or practice that would be considered spiritual or religious groups or cults? If YES, please explain. These are areas which may have impacted you on a deeper spiritual level than you realize and are important to recognize if there were harmful doors opened in your life.

_____
_____
_____
_____

MENTAL, EMOTIONAL AND TRAUMA HISTORY

Have there been any major traumas in your life? _____
_____

Which of the following have you struggled with or had difficulty controlling?
Doubts _____ Compulsive thoughts _____ Blasphemous thoughts _____
Chronic Pain _____ Dizziness _____ Fear of death _____
PMS _____ Headaches _____ Fear of losing mind _____
Anger _____ Loneliness _____ Fear of suicide _____ Anxiety _____ Depression
Fear of hurting loved ones _____ Insecurity _____ Obsessive thoughts _____
Frustration _____ Worthlessness _____ Hatred _____ Lustful thoughts _____
Fantasy _____ Daydreaming _____

MORAL CLIMATE

During the first 18 years of life, how would you rate the moral atmosphere in which you were raised?

	Overly Permissive	Permissive	Average	Strict	Overly Strict
Clothing	1	2	3	4	5
Sex	1	2	3	4	5
Dating	1	2	3	4	5
Movies	1	2	3	4	5
Literature	1	2	3	4	5
Free will	1	2	3	4	5
Drinking	1	2	3	4	5
Smoking	1	2	3	4	5
Church attendance	1	2	3	4	5

References List

Lesson One:
- Sexual Behavior in the Human Male, Sexual Behavior in Human Female by Alfred C. Kinsey. Wardell B. Pomeroy, Clyde E. Martin, Paul H. Gebhard and W. B. Saunders, Philadelphia, (1953©).
- Kinsey, Sex and Fraud, by Dr. Judith A. Reisman, Edward Eichel, Huntington House Publishers, 1990.
- Harvard Law School, Christopher Columbus Langdell
- President of Harvard Univ., Charles W. Eliot…concept led to Darwin's theory of evolution which led to secular humanism. 1870–1960s—sex education in the USA.
- Pew Research Center analysis of AU.S. Census Bureau data. (2017)—Children living with solo mom Pew Research Center Census data.
- Statistics about Children from single-parent homes. (U.S. Centers for Disease Control)—(CDC) and the Guttmacher Institute. —Abortion).
- Centers for Disease Control and Prevention (CDC) WISQARS Leading Causes of Death Reports in 2016. Suicidal Thoughts and Behaviors Among U.S. Adults 2016—Courtesy of SAMHSA.
- Mental Health Facts by Mental Health America
- Drug Abuse and Addiction reports by National Institute on Drug Abuse
- Pornography by United Families.org. J**Lesson Two:**
- FUTURE WAR OF THE CHURCH by Chuck D. Pierce and Rebeca Wagner Systema
- Principalities Over Families (Commentary made available by http://www.answersIngenesisorg/creation/v20/13/china.asp© 2005 Answers in Genesis)
- "A Child Called "It" by Dave Pelzer (Health Communications, Inc., Deerfield Beach, Fla., ©1995 (1)
- Born Only Once, intra-womb bonding—copyright by Dr. Conrad Barrs, M.D.
- ICA Theory (Inclusion+ Control + Affect) Design by Proctor & Gamble for Personal Growth and Development Training event, 1970's (Millie McCarty)

Lesson Three:
- Tree of Bondage vs. Tree of Freedom—diagram—source unknown

Lesson Four:
- Family Systems Model—Best reference: Bowen Family Systems Theory materials. My material came from my workshop notes from a training class for Human Growth & Development Training by Procter-Gamble Industry, 1975–76.
- Family Systems Model—Best reference: Bowen Family Systems Theory materials. My material came from my workshop notes from a training class for Human Growth & Development Training by Procter-Gamble Industry, 1975–76.

Lesson Five:
- FOUR BASIC TYPES OF FAMILIES—from conference notes 1980s. Best resource: Bowen Family Systems Theory, Peter Titleman, Ph.D. © 1990)

Lesson Six:
- Other Altars, Craig Lockwood, pages 231–232, How trauma affects the developmental stages of the brain).
- Alan Shores, Professor at UCLA—Developing Core Self-Bonding, brain image studies in relation to ADHD and ADD.
- Jean Illsley-Clarke and Connie Dawson, authors of Growing Up Again, Hazelden Education, ©1989.
- Child Development Chart (Erikson + Erikson & Clarke Combined charts. Source: Growing Up Again by Clarke and Connie Dawson, Hazelden Educ. © 1992. Servant Publications

Lesson Seven:
- THE GENOGRAM—Best resource: Genograms in Family Assessment by Monica McGoldrick & Randy Gerson, Norton Publishing, ©1985.

Lesson Eight:
- (Madison 721@aol.com, AOL Friedrich Nietzsche—Existentialism, www.age-of-the-sage.org/philosophy/nietzsche.html)
- Protecting the Self: Defense Mechanisms in Action by Phoebe Cramer, Ph.D. ©2002

Lesson Nine:
- The Lies We Believe by Dr. Chris Thurman, Thomas Nelson, Copyright, © 2002
- GOD'S PERCEPTION VS. MY PERCEPTION—unknown source
- "Other Altars" by Craig Lockwood, Compcare Publishers, 1993
- Ishbane's Conspiracy by Randy Alcorn

Lesson Eleven:
- Johari Window—Developed by Joseph Luft and Harry Ingham, 1955 www.copmmunicationskills/johariwindow-model
- Diagram—Neuron activity in the Hippocampus (Internet Source Unknown)
- Drawing of Prefrontal Cortex, the Hippocampus and Lymbic System and their functions. (Internet Source Unknown)
- Cycle of Dysfunction—Adapted by Millie McCarty from the Cycle of Sin and Addiction—by Patrick Carnes, Out of the Shadows, Understanding Sexual Addiction, ©1994, Net Library, Inc.

Lesson Twelve:
- The Iceberg Theory—Hidden Evidence of unresolved conflict Internet Source—What is the Iceberg theory? —Embrace yourself, embrace the world (embrace-yourself-embrace-the-world.com)
- Cycle of Sin and Addiction Cyclical Terms—Out of the Shadows, Understanding Sexual Addiction, By Patrick Carnes, ©1994, Net Library, Inc.
- CYCLE OF SIN AND ADDICTION CHART—Adapted from Out of the Shadows, Understanding Sexual Addiction, By Patrick Carnes, ©1994, Net Library, Inc.

Lesson Thirteen:
- Drs. Henry Cloud and John Townsend, authors of Healthy Boundaries, 1992 ©Zondervan

Lesson Fourteen:
- Josh McDowell (Right from Wrong, Word Publishing, ©1994
- Total Forgiveness by R. T. Kendall, ©2002, Charisma House
- "Saying" (Source Unknown)

Note:
- All scriptures are taken from the King James Version of the bible

Don't let your perceptions keep you in bondage!!!!!

Our Systematic Process of Resolving

Unresolved Conflict Eternally

SPRUCE

Provides faith-based processes and proven psychological assessment tools that "get to the root" of the problem and resolves the mental conflict!

INT'L INSTITUTE FOR TRAUMA RECOVERY

Millie McCarty, M.A., LPCC, Author, Pastor, Founder, CEO

www.ingramcontent.com/pod-product-compliance
Lightning Source LLC
Chambersburg PA
CBHW081204020426
42333CB00020B/2623